Social Development and the Adolescent

A Landmark School Teaching Guide

Cheryl K. Iannucci

Landmark School, Inc.
Prides Crossing, MA

Landmark School, Inc.

Published by Landmark School, Inc.
P.O. Box 227
Prides Crossing, MA 01965

Library of Congress Cataloging-in-Publication Data

Library of Congress Card Number: 00-112056
    ISBN 0-9624119-5-7

Printed in the United States of America

Landmark School, Inc.

Contents

Landmark School, Inc.

Preface

Adolescents with learning disabilities are at high risk of developing insecure, under-valuing, inaccurate perceptions of themselves both physically and psychologically. The resulting poor image and low self-esteem predisposes them to engage in such negative behaviors as substance abuse, poorly judged social interactions, and premature sex. The strategies and exercises in this book are designed to help adolescents with learning disabilities deal more positively with the extremely damaging and socially wasteful effects of that uncontrollable combination of being young and learning disabled.

Social Development and the Adolescent: A Landmark School Teaching Guide introduces an interactive approach to social skill-building. It is my hope that this curriculum helps teachers incorporate the adaptive behavior and readiness training necessary for students with learning disabilities to interact successfully in their social environments. The strategies and exercises in this guide have proven successful with language-impaired adolescents in grades eight through twelve. Teachers and counselors can use this guide to interact with adolescents with learning disabilities and teach them social skills with a new effectiveness.

Landmark School, Inc.

Acknowledgments

I would like to thank and acknowledge the generous support of The Margaret Hall Foundation.

I would also like to thank the many individuals and organizations that helped make the publication of *Social Development and the Adolescent: A Landmark School Teaching Guide* possible.

I appreciate the long-standing interest, support, and efforts of Charles Harris, Patricia Peterman, Cliff Irons, Chris Murphy, and Henry Willette of the Landmark School. Also, Health Quarters and Help for Abused Women and Their Children (HAWC)—through their educational presentations and materials—contributed ideas to this work. William Galiano, Charles Harris, Suzanne Crossman, and Karen Wilk helped with editing.

I would especially like to thank my husband and parents for their encouragement and ongoing support.

Please forgive my omission of explicit thanks to the many others who have helped make this book possible.

About The Author

Cheryl K. Iannucci, M.S.Ed., has been with Landmark School since 1992. Cheryl served as director of Landmark School's Women's Program and as the assistant dean of students; she is currently a Guidance Counselor. She has presented workshops on social issues to teachers, students, and parents. Prior to her employment at Landmark School, Cheryl was employed by the Commonwealth of Massachusetts, Department of Social Services, and Pressley Ridge Youth Development Extension in West Virginia as a social worker. She is a 1989 graduate of Bethany College, where she received her Bachelor's degree in Psychology, and a 2000 graduate of Simmons College, where she received her M.S.Ed.

Landmark School, Inc.

About the Landmark School

Founded in 1971, the Landmark School is recognized as an international leader in the field of language-based learning disabilities. The School is a co-educational boarding and day school with students, 7 to 20 years old, from across the United States and around the world. Within its highly structured living and learning environment, Landmark offers individualized instruction to elementary, middle and high school students. The School's program emphasizes the development of language and learning skills. Landmark students learn strategies for managing their learning differences so that they can realize their full potential both socially and academically.

About The Landmark School Outreach Program

Established in 1977, the Landmark School Outreach Program provides professional development programs and publications that offer practical and effective strategies that help children learn. These strategies are based on Landmark's Six Teaching Principles and on over thirty years experience in the classroom. Members of the Landmark Faculty deliver graduate courses and seminars at the Landmark Outreach Center and on-site at school districts across the country. For more information about professional development opportunities and publications, visit our website at *http://www.landmarkschool.org* or contact the Landmark School Outreach Program at (978) 236–3216.

Landmark School, Inc.

Landmark Teaching Principles

Imagine . . . an instructional hour in which all students are interested and involved. The teacher motivates students by making the material meaningful to them. Information is presented in a variety of interesting ways that engage the range of learning styles in the class. The teacher builds opportunities for success by presenting information in small, sequential steps, and offers positive feedback as soon as students learn and apply a relevant new skill. The teacher provides examples and clear directions for homework, and sets aside a few minutes at the end of class for students to begin the homework assignment. During this time, the teacher answers questions and makes sure each student understands the task. In short, the teacher structures the hour so each student is challenged, works at an appropriate level, and leaves the class feeling successful and confident.

The Landmark School was founded in 1971 to provide this type of structured, success-oriented instruction to students with learning disabilities. For more than thirty years, Landmark teachers have continually enhanced and refined teaching strategies to help students learn more effectively. Landmark has shared its teaching strategies with public- and private-school teachers from all over the world through Landmark seminars. All students can and do learn from Landmark's structured and success-oriented instructional models.

At the heart of Landmark's instructional strategies and programs are six teaching principles:

Provide Opportunities for Success
Providing students with opportunities for success is key. Failure and poor self-esteem often result when teachers challenge students beyond their ability. Landmark begins teaching students at their current level of ability. This approach improves basic skills and enhances confidence. As Landmark teachers introduce each new skill, they provide basic examples and assignments to build confidence and keep students from becoming overwhelmed. As the information becomes more challenging, teachers assign students easier problems to supplement the more difficult ones. In this way, those students who are having trouble with the material complete at least part of the assignment while they work at understanding and learning

Landmark School, Inc.

to apply new information. Teachers give themselves permission to provide students with whatever structure is necessary to help students be successful, such as study guides for tests, templates for writing, and guidelines for projects. Only with a solid foundation of basic skills and confidence can students make progress. That is why it is key to provide them with opportunities for success.

Use Multi-Sensory Approaches

Multi-sensory teaching is effective for all students. In general, it means presenting all information to students via three sensory modalities: visual, auditory, and tactile. Visual presentation techniques include graphic organizers for structuring writing and pictures for reinforcing instruction; auditory presentation techniques include conducting thorough discussions and reading aloud; tactile presentation techniques include manipulating blocks and creating paragraphs about objects students can hold in their hands. Overall, implementing a multi-sensory approach to teaching is not difficult; in fact, many teachers use such an approach. It is important, however, to be aware of the three sensory modes and to plan to integrate them every day.

Micro-Unit and Structure Tasks

Effective teaching involves breaking information down into its smallest units and providing clear guidelines for all assignments. This is especially important for students with learning disabilities. "Micro-uniting" and structuring are elements of directive teaching, which Landmark consistently uses with students. Micro-uniting means analyzing the parts of a task or assignment and teaching those parts one step at a time. Teachers organize information so that students can see and follow the steps clearly and sequentially. As students learn to micro-unit for themselves, they become less likely to give up on tasks that appear confusing or overwhelming. Consequently, these strategies enable students to proceed in a step-by-step, success-oriented way.

Ensure Automatization through Practice and Review

Automatization is the process of learning and assimilating a task or skill so completely that it can be consistently completed with little or no conscious attention. Repetition and review (spiraling) are critical. Sometimes students appear to understand a concept, only to forget it a day, week, or month later. It is not until students have automatized a skill that they can effectively remember and use it as a foundation for new tasks. Teachers must therefore provide ample opportunities for students to repeat and review learned material. For example, the Landmark writing process emphasizes practice and consistency. Students always brainstorm, map/outline, draft, and proofread in the same way. This provides them with an ongoing, consistent review of learned skills.

Provide Models

Providing models is simple, yet very important. It is one of the most effective teaching techniques. Models are concrete examples of what teachers expect. They do not mean that teachers are doing assignments for students. They are standards to which students can compare their own work. A model or example of a completed assignment serves as a springboard for students to begin the assignment. For example, teachers should give students a model of a sequential paragraph when teaching basic sequential paragraph writing.

Include Students in the Learning Process

Students are not passive receptacles to fill with information. They come to class with their own frames of reference. Their unique experiences and knowledge affect them as learners and should be taken into account. Therefore, during every exercise, teachers should accept student input as much as possible. They should justify assignments, accept suggestions, solicit ideas, and provide ample time for students to share ideas. Teachers should include students in assessing their own progress by reviewing test results, written reports, and educational plans. Creating and improvising opportunities to involve students in the learning process allows students to become aware of how they learn and why certain skills benefit them. As a result, students are motivated and more likely to apply those skills when working independently. In short, an included student becomes an invested student who is eager to learn.

Introduction

Adolescence in today's society is a developmental challenge all its own. Add a learning disability, and the challenge is nothing less than extraordinary.

As Assistant Dean of Students and Guidance Counselor at Landmark School, it has been my privilege to work with students with language-based learning disabilities—as well as parents, school administrators, community organizations, and other citizens—on the challenges confronting adolescents today.

Young people are experiencing persistent difficulty coping with the pressures placed upon them—pressures that arise in considerable measure from their developmental changes, peer pressure, and experiences with dating and relationships. These experiences are more difficult for adolescents with learning disabilities because of their inability to process both incoming information and their own feelings appropriately. Students with learning disabilities often misperceive social interactions, distort information, have difficulty recognizing or interpreting verbal and non-verbal cues, and fail to grasp the nuances of complex interpersonal issues.

Social Development and the Adolescent: A Landmark School Teaching Guide blends instructional and cooperative learning with interactive exercises to motivate students and broaden their knowledge while learning social skills. Students are encouraged to participate in their own learning process. The curriculum includes exercises specifically designed to enhance the social development of adolescents with learning disabilities. Instructions to teachers, with examples, show how to integrate ideas and concepts into exercises.

Landmark School, Inc.

Discovering Yourself

Overview

Unit 1, Discovering Yourself, offers students an opportunity to explore their feelings about themselves. They learn to reflect upon their feelings and personal thoughts. Students examine the origins of their belief systems, evaluate their personal beliefs and attitudes, and establish a sense of self-respect. Students also examine societal influences on body image.

Objectives

Upon completion of this unit, students will be better able to:

- describe some of their feelings
- describe the impact of their thinking on their personal attitudes
- state that others have similar attitudes about themselves
- develop a realistic image of their bodies

Materials

Handouts: What Do You Think about Yourself?

List of Feelings

Defense Mechanisms Definitions

Defense Mechanisms Worksheet

Respecting Yourself

Displays: Pictures of athletes, supermodels, and people in various other roles

Equipment: Blackboard, whiteboard, or easel with flip chart

1

Instructions

Step 1   Post pictures of athletes, supermodels, and people in different roles around the classroom. Distribute all handouts for the unit.

Step 2   Tell students that this unit is designed to help them look at how they feel about themselves. Our inner selves are our personalities, attitudes, and feelings; our outer selves are our physical selves or appearances. Often, we allow others to influence how we feel about ourselves.

Explain that, over the next several days, you will be encouraging students to evaluate their feelings about who they are. By knowing ourselves, we can better understand our feelings about ourselves and others, as well as how we feel about and respond to different situations. Answer any questions students have about the unit.

Step 3   Tell students that they are going to start exploring their feelings about themselves by completing a questionnaire, What Do You Think about Yourself? There are no right or wrong answers. The answer to each question is based on how each student feels. (Depending on the level of the students, you may need to define words used in question #7, on personal attributes.)

Step 4   Ask for feedback from students about their answers.

Step 5   Ask students to write one to two paragraphs that describe who they are. (This can be done in class or as homework.)

Step 6   Invite students to brainstorm feelings they experience from time to time. Write the feelings students name on the board. Invite students to describe situations in which they had the feelings they name. Some students may find it difficult to talk about themselves. You may want to offer students the option of talking about an anonymous friend's feelings and experiences.

Step 7   Divide students into small groups. Ask each group to develop a skit that expresses at least five of the feelings on the List of Feelings. Depending on the level of the students, you may need to review words from the list.

Step 8   Ask each group to act out its skit for the class.

Step 9   When everyone is back in their seats, explain that we've all experienced hurt at some time. As a result of hurt feelings, we can develop what are called defense mechanisms. Defense mechanisms are a way to protect ourselves from hurt. In other words, defense mechanisms are our protective armor. While they help reduce our anxiety, they can also inhibit our growth. They can interfere with our ability to interact and develop relationships with others.

Step 10 Review the terms on the handout, Defense Mechanisms Definitions. Give examples of how we use defense mechanisms for protection.

Step 11 Ask students to complete the worksheet, Defense Mechanisms Worksheet. When they are finished, answer any questions.

Step 12 Explain the importance of listening to our inner thoughts and feelings and being able to acknowledge why we respond to situations the way we do. Tell students that the way we respond to situations may be based on our prior experiences. For example, people who have been abused are more likely to abuse others. A different type of example is that when a friend violates our trust, we may be less likely to share private information with that person.

Step 13 Ask students to define, in their own words, the word respect. Discuss the difference between respect for others and self-respect. Tell students that respecting ourselves means paying attention to how we feel, what we need, and what we want. Let students know that it is OK and important to pay attention to how we feel. Before we can respect others and establish solid relationships, we must respect and feel comfortable with ourselves.

Step 14 Review each letter on the RESPECT poster and what it stands for.

Step 15 Using the handout, Respecting Yourself, review ways to achieve selfrespect, as follows.

- We evaluate our feelings by assessing our inner thoughts and determining what we need and want.

- We become assertive by learning to express our needs. Unit 4 is dedicated to assertiveness training.

- Short-term goals are goals we can reasonably achieve within a short time. Short-term goals help us achieve long-term goals. For example, a short-term goal might be to prepare for an exam.

- Long-term goals are goals we set while looking towards the future. For example, a long-term goal may be to go to college or to be an engineer.

- We establish what's good for us by noticing what makes us feel positive about ourselves and pursuing those things.

- We advocate for what we need and want by asserting ourselves appropriately and stating our position or desire.

- We never do anything that makes us feel uncomfortable. This is the most important step. We must respect ourselves and listen to our inner thoughts. If the inner thought is "no," we say "no" We don't let anyone persuade or force us to do something we do not want to do.

Before students can establish healthy relationships with others, they must learn to like and respect themselves. They must pay attention to their own needs, thoughts, and desires.

What Do You Think About Yourself?

The questions below ask how you feel about yourself. There are no right or wrong answers.

1. **I am comfortable with myself.**

   always   often   sometimes   never

2. **I like my personality.**

   always   often   sometimes   never

3. **I am comfortable with my overall physical appearance.**

   always   often   sometimes   never

4. **I am comfortable with my weight.**

   always   often   sometimes   never

5. **How much weight would you like to gain?**

   none   5 to 10 lbs.   10 to 15 lbs.   15 to 20 lbs.   20 + lbs.

6. **How much weight would you like to lose?**

   none   5 to 10 lbs.   10 to 15 lbs.   15 to 20 lbs.   20 + lbs.

7. **Which of the following personal attributes do you possess?
   Check as many as you want.**

friendly	caring	understanding	good-looking
a good attitude	a poor attitude	assertive	passive
aggressive	strong-willed	empathetic	trustworthy
kind	generous	strong	weak
flexible	happy		

8. **If you had the opportunity, what would you change?**

   nothing   attitude   personality   appearance

9. **My goal in life is to become:**

10. **To reach my goal, I must:**

List Of Feelings

Accepted	Disgusted	Proud
Affectionate	Disrespectful	Rejected
Afraid	Distant	Relaxed
Angry	Distrustful	Relieved
Annoyed	Embarrassed	Respectful
Anxious	Envious	Sad
Ashamed	Excited	Safe
Betrayed	Guilty	Satisfied
Calm	Happy	Scared
Carefree	Hopeful	Shy
Close	Hurt	Sorry
Comfortable	Jealous	Special
Confident	Lonely	Tense
Confused	Lost	Thankful
Contented	Loving	Trusting
Defensive	Neglected	Uncomfortable
Dependent	Nervous	Uptight
Depressed	Paralyzed	Worried
Devastated	Peaceful	
Disappointed	Protective	

Defense Mechanisms Definitions

Defense mechanisms are the ways in which we protect ourselves from hurt. While defense mechanisms reduce our anxiety, they can also inhibit our growth and interfere with our ability to interact with others.

1. **Repression** is when we exclude from our awareness any thoughts, feelings, or wishes that could threaten us. A panic attack is the experience of being overwhelmed with anxiety when a repressed memory comes out. (Panic attacks usually occur when we are tired.)

2. **Regression** is when we resolve difficulties by going back to a behavior that was satisfying at an earlier age but that we've since outgrown.

3. **Projection** is when we attribute to others our own unacceptable impulses or desires. We can't admit to our feelings, so we blame others.

4. A **reaction formation** is when we protect ourselves from dangerous desires by not only repressing them, but by developing conscious attitudes and behavior patterns that are just the opposite.

5. **Emotional insulation** is when we reduce the tensions of anxiety by withdrawing into a shell of passivity.

6. A **fantasy** is a construction of the ideal world—the world as we'd like it to be. A good fantasy can motivate you, but it's dangerous to lose yourself in a fantasy.

7. **Compensation** is when we attempt to make up for our real or imagined personal defects or weaknesses by going overboard in an area where we are successful.

8. **Identification** is when we reduce anxiety and build up our self-concept by attributing to ourselves the achievements, status, and characteristics of another person or group.

9. **Rationalization** is when we give alternative reasons for our behavior to conceal from ourselves and others the real reasons for that behavior.

10. **Displacement** is when we shift our emotions from the person to whom they are directed to another person.

Defense Mechanisms Worksheet

1. **Repression:**

   Example:

2. **Regression:**

   Example:

3. **Projection:**

   Example:

4. **Reaction formation:**

   Example:

5. **Emotional insulation:**

   Example:

6. **Fantasy:**

   Example:

7. **Compensation:**

   Example:

8. **Identification:**

   Example:

9. **Rationalization:**

   Example:

10. **Displacement:**

    Example:

Respecting Yourself

Respecting yourself means paying attention to how you feel, what you need, and what you want.

R is for responsibility to yourself.

E is for the expectations you set for yourself.

S is for keeping yourself safe.

P is for perseverance.

E is for your willingness to endure what's thrown your way.

C is for your commitment to yourself.

T is for trusting yourself.

Ways To Achieve Self-Respect

- Evaluate your feelings.
- Learn to become assertive.
- Set short-term goals.
- Set long-term goals.
- Establish what's good for you.
- Advocate for what you need and want.
- Never do anything that makes you feel uncomfortable.

Before you can respect others and establish solid relationships, you must respect and feel comfortable with yourself.

Communicating

Overview

Unit 2, Communicating, helps students communicate with others in social situations. Students review ways in which information becomes distorted. They learn to recognize and understand verbal and non-verbal cues. Students also learn methods to help them process both incoming information and their own feelings appropriately and effectively.

Objectives

Upon completion of this unit, students will be better able to:

- recognize and understand verbal and non-verbal cues
- describe the ways in which we distort our thoughts
- process social interactions before drawing conclusions
- simplify complex situations
- interact with others in appropriate ways

Materials

Handouts: What Affects Communication?

Ten Ways We Distort Our Thoughts

Questions to Ask Yourself When Communicating

Verbal and Non-Verbal Cues

Non-Verbal Cues

Non-Verbal Behavior Worksheet

Equipment: Blackboard, whiteboard, or easel with flip chart

Landmark School, Inc.

Instructions

Step 1   Distribute all handouts for this unit.

Step 2   Begin by explaining the importance of effective communication and how communication affects our social, professional, and private lives.

Step 3   Invite students to brainstorm factors that affect communication. Refer to the handout, What Affects Communication? Briefly discuss how each factor influences the communication process. For example, when we have recently had a negative experience interacting with someone, we may not feel comfortable approaching that person and having an open conversation.

Step 4   Explain that how we feel about ourselves, others, and certain situations can interfere with how we perceive situations or conversations. In fact, ninety percent of our problems are caused by our own thoughts. Review the handout, Ten Ways We Distort Our Thoughts, including one or more examples of each.

Step 5   State that before we communicate with others, we need to ask ourselves certain questions. Review the handout, Questions to Ask Yourself When Communicating. These questions are to help students evaluate the communication process and figure out the best time and place to communicate what they want.

Step 6   Distinguish between verbal and non-verbal communication. State that people communicate both verbally and non-verbally. Review the handout, Verbal and Non-Verbal Cues. Invite students to brainstorm additional verbal and non-verbal cues. You can run a game in which students role play non-verbal cues and other students name the cue.

Step 7   Explain that certain non-verbal cues can mean different things. For example, laughter can mean that someone is happy, embarrassed, uncomfortable and nervous, or doesn't know how else to respond.

Step 8   Review the handout, Non-Verbal Cues. Explain the different types of non-verbal cues, emphasizing the importance of each. You may view a video or a taped sitcom and ask students to identify the meaning of some non-verbal cues.

Step 9   Review the directions to the Non-Verbal Behavior Worksheet, emphasizing that students can assign more than one feeling to each description of a behavior. (You can assign this worksheet as homework.)

Step 10   Review students' answers to the Non-Verbal Behavior Worksheet. You may have volunteers role play the non-verbal cues as others report their answers.

Step 11   Involve the class in planning and implementing a social event, such as a school dance or social hour. Ask students to keep a journal to document the process. Students should record their communications with authority figures and peers, issues that arose, and how they could improve the process next time.

Additional Activity

- Develop role plays for the different types of non-verbal and verbal cues.

What Affects Communication?

- Preferences, prejudices, biases, and experiences
- Type of relationship
- Self-doubt, stress level, value systems, and knowledge
- Time of day, amount of sleep, and health
- Environment
- Personal issues, differences, and comfort level
- Gender and race
- Sexual orientation, and cultural differences
- Facial expressions
- Dress and hair style
- Listening (or not listening)

Ten Ways We Distort Our Thoughts

1. **All-or-nothing thinking** is black-and-white thinking. It seeks perfection. It is unrealistic.

2. **Over-generalizing** is believing that something will happen over and over because it happened once.

3. **Mental filtering** is picking out a negative detail in a situation and dwelling on it until the whole situation appears negative.

4. **Disqualifying the positive** is when we turn something positive into a negative. For example, if Susan compliments Jill on her appearance and Jill says, "Oh, you're just saying that," then Jill is disqualifying the positive.

5. **Jumping to conclusions** is when we jump to a negative result, either by making assumptions (mind-reading) or making negative predictions.

6. **Magnifying and minimizing** are when we perceive things out of proportion. We exaggerate (magnify) them or dismiss (minimize) them.

7. **Emotional reasoning** is when we interpret our emotions as truths and make it hard for others to convince us otherwise.

8. **"Should" statements** are when we motivate ourselves by what we feel we should and shouldn't do. It's as if we believe we should be punished for doing or not doing certain things.

9. **Labeling** is when we create a completely negative self-image based on our errors. This is self-defeating and irrational thinking.

10. **Personalizing** is when we assume responsibility (guilt) for negative events or treatment beyond our control.

    Ninety percent of our problems are caused by our own thoughts!

Questions To Ask Yourself When Communicating

Ask yourself the questions below to evaluate the communication process and figure out the best time and place to communicate what you want.

1. What do you need to communicate?

2. Why do you want to communicate? For example, do you want to resolve conflict? prevent conflict? change a situation? express concern?

3. What is the best way to communicate what you want? Is a verbal or a written communication preferable?

4. What is the best time and place to communicate what you want? For example, is it best communicated at home? over the phone? at school? before school? after school?

5. Is the person I want to communicate with open and in the right mood for the communication to be successful?

6. Are there others around who might interfere with the communication? Are there others around who might make me or the person I want to communicate with feel uncomfortable? How will I recognize if others are or become uncomfortable?

Verbal and Non-Verbal Cues

Verbal Cues	Non-Verbal Cues
"Yes."	Head nodding up and down; smiling
"No."	Head shaking side to side; growing quiet; withdrawing
"I'm uncomfortable."	Backing or walking away; growing quiet; beginning to laugh
"I'm in a good mood."	Smiling; looking peaceful and content
"I'm upset."	Grimacing; growing quiet; holding the body very rigidly
"I'm embarrassed."	Growing red in the face; laughing; withdrawing
"I'm shy."	Being quiet; being reserved; not participating in the activity conversation

Non-Verbal Cues

1. **Touch**

    - Touch someone only if the situation is comfortable.

    - Do not use touch if someone pulls away.

    - Do not use touch if your meaning can be taken sexually.

2. **Body language, including facial gestures, hand and leg movements, sitting positions, and eye contact.**

    - Body language is very important in communicating.

    - It delivers additional information beyond what we say.

    - It allows us to see what someone really feels.

    - While words can be faked, body language is difficult to fake.

3. **Tone of voice**

    - Our tone of voice escalates as we become excited or upset.

4. **Speed of speech**

    - We speak faster when we are nervous or excited.

    - We speak slower when we are upset or down.

5. **Personal space**

    - Personal space is the distance we maintain between ourselves and the people with whom we communicate.

    - People who do not know each other well generally maintain more personal space.

Non-Verbal Behavior Worksheet

Please review the non-verbal behaviors listed on the left, and match them with feelings from the list on the right. You can list more than one feeling for each non-verbal behavior.

Column A

_____ Leslie's eyes are teary.

_____ Victoria sighs.

_____ Paula sits very straight and rigid in a chair, making no direct eye contact.

_____ Jane seems silly. She laughs at inappropriate times.

_____ Kelly's face is tightly drawn and her lips are pursed. She seems to be glaring at you Her face is slightly flushed.

_____ Emily takes a comfortable position in a chair next to you Her face is relaxed, and she looks directly at you. Her voice is loud enough for you to hear. She speaks a rate that seems natural.

_____ Joyce sits very straight and rigid in her chair. She does not look directly at you. Her lips are tight and when she speaks, it is in a high-pitched voice. She speaks very rapidly.

_____ Denise, a new student, talks very softly, choosing words with great care. She avoids eye contact and says very little.

Column B

1. Uncomfortable

2. Anxious

3. Shy

4. Angry

5. Comfortable

6. Sad

7. Relaxed

8. Tense

9. Embarrassed

10. Happy

11. Relieved

Making Decisions

Overview

Unit 3, Making Decisions, explores the decision-making process. Students learn questions to ask themselves when making decisions. They also learn to evaluate the positive and negative consequences of their decisions. After students learn to make a well-considered decision, they learn to follow through.

Objectives

Upon completion of this unit, students will be better able to:

- describe the thought process that goes into making a decision
- understand that every decision has a consequence
- apply an evaluation process to make decisions that are right for them
- understand the importance of following through with decisions

Materials

Handouts: Ask Yourself Some Questions

Thought Process Worksheet

Displays: How to Follow Through

Equipment: Blackboard, whiteboard, or easel with flip chart

Instructions

Step 1   Display How to Follow Through. Distribute all handouts for the unit.

Step 2   Begin by asking students to brainstorm situations in which they might need to make a tough decision (for example, whether to use substances or have sex). Write the situations on the board.

Step 3   Tell students that this unit is designed to help them make quality decisions. They'll learn specific methods for identifying and weighing all the options around a decision. The goal is for them to be able to make decisions they are comfortable with. Emphasize that the intent is not to influence students' decisions, but to help them make decisions that are in their best interests.

Step 4   Divide students into small groups. Instruct each group to pick a reporter. Assign one situation from the brainstorming list (step 2) to each group. Ask the groups to make a decision on their situation using the handout, Ask Yourself Some Questions. Groups do not need to reach consensus.

Step 5   Ask each reporter to share her group's results and decision-making process.

Step 6   Referencing the Thought Process Worksheet, draw a thought process diagram on the board. Brainstorm options for one or two of the sample situations. With the class, develop a list of the positive and negative consequences of each option. For example:

Options	Positive Consequences	Negative Consequences
Abstain	No pregnancy	No intimacy
Have sex	Experience sex	Sexually transmitted disease; pregnancy; guilt

Step 7   Instruct students to select a situation that is affecting their lives (or a friend's life), consider it carefully, and review their options. The next step is to write down the positive and negative consequences of each option using the format on the Thought Process Worksheet. (You can give this as an in-class or homework assignment.)

Step 8   Ask for volunteers to review their situations and thought processes. If appropriate, invite the class to support volunteers by offering further options or consequences.

Step 9   Reference the display, How to Follow Through. Explain the importance of following through with decisions.

Step 10   Divide students into small groups. Assign each group a situation from the brainstorming list or another scenario. Ask each group to act out the situation using one "no" method from How to Follow Through.

Ask Yourself Some Questions

Before you make a decision, it is important to ask yourself some questions. For example:

- What is my reason for making this decision?

- Will this decision affect my relationship with anyone else, such as my friends or parents?

- Have I thought about all the possible consequences of this decision?

- Am I willing to accept all the consequences?

- Do I have the knowledge to make a good decision?

- Can I make this decision without any guilt or regrets?

- Are there more comfortable ways of accomplishing similar goals?

- Does this decision go against my religious beliefs?

- Have I honestly considered my values?

- Do I want to make this decision because of pressure from my friends?

Remember, you are the only one who can answer these questions. You need to think carefully and be willing to ask for help or advice.

Thought Process Worksheet

Options	Positive Consequences	Negative Consequences

How To Follow Through

1. Decide what you want to do about the situation at a time when you feel good about yourself. Talk to someone about your options. Make your decision at a time when you do not feel pressured.

2. Decide in advance what guidelines you have established for yourself regarding the decision.

3. Tell whomever may be affected by your decision in advance and make yourself very clear. Do not wait until the last minute to tell someone your decision.

4. Avoid high-pressure situations. Do not place yourself in a situation in which you feel obligated or pressured to change your mind.

5. If your answer is no, state it clearly.

Ways To Say "No"

Method	Examples
Simple no	"No, thanks." "No."
Emphatic no	"No! I don't want to do that!"
Repetitive no	"No. No. No."
Turn the table	"You say that if I were your friend, I would. But if you were my friend, you wouldn't insist."
State your feelings	"I don't feel comfortable doing _____." "I have decided not to _____."
Leave the situation	Walk away.
Steer clear	If you suspect a high-pressure situation, avoid the pressure by avoiding the situation.
Call in the cavalry	Tell the person you will tell someone in authority or power, such as a counselor, parent, or staff member.
Safety in numbers	Keep a friend who supports your decision close by.

Assertiveness Training

Overview

Unit 4, Assertiveness Training, teaches students to assert themselves to fulfill their own physiological and psychological needs. Students learn appropriate, effective ways to advocate for what they need and want.

Objectives

Upon completion of this unit, students will be better able to:

- distinguish between assertiveness and aggressiveness
- advocate effectively for their own needs and desires

Materials

Handouts: What Would You Do?

What Would You Do? Questionnaire Outcomes

Learn to Become Assertive

Passive, Assertive, or Aggressive?

Assertiveness Role Plays

Displays: Billie Jean King quote (see Step 6)

Equipment: Blackboard, whiteboard, or easel with flip chart

Video camera (optional)

Landmark School, Inc.

Instructions

Step 1 Display the Billie Jean King quote. Distribute the handouts for this unit, except for What Would You Do? Questionnaire Outcomes

Step 2 Start this unit by explaining the importance of assertiveness. We need to assert ourselves in certain situations to fulfill our physiological and psychological needs.

Briefly define and distinguish between physiological (physical) and psychological (emotional) needs, if necessary. For example, a student who requires a lower bunk bed due to a medical condition has a physiological need. A student who requires a lower bunk because she is afraid of falling out of bed has a psychological need. Both types of needs are valid.

Step 3 Ask students to answer the multiple-choice questions on the questionnaire, What Would You Do? State that there are no right or wrong answers. Students should answer based on how they would personally respond to each situation. Emphasize that the exercise is only to help students learn more about themselves.

Step 4 Explain the questionnaire scoring scale, as follows:

- one point for each "a" answer

- two points for each "b" answer

- three points for each "c" answer

Ask students to tally up their scores.

Step 5 Distribute the handout, What Would You Do? Questionnaire Outcomes. Explain the scoring categories, as follows:

- Students who score from fourteen to eighteen points are in the assertive category.

- Students who score from nine to thirteen points are in the aggressive category.

- Students who score from zero to eight points are in the passive category.

Step 6 Read the displayed quote from Billie Jean King: "To change or not to change is a risk. You must trust and listen to yourself. Sometimes not changing is a bigger risk than change."

Step 7 Distinguish between assertiveness, passivity, and aggressiveness. Use the handout, Learn to Become Assertive, and the worksheet, Passive, Assertive, or Aggressive?

Step 8 Invite students to brainstorm situations in which they need to be assertive. Write the situations on the blackboard or easel. For each situation, discuss what might happen if students didn't assert themselves. Moderate a discussion about why it can be easier to be aggressive or passive than assertive.

Step 9 Divide students into small groups. Assign each group one role play from the handout, Assertiveness Role Plays. Give groups five to ten minutes to develop a skit for the role play.

Step 10 Invite the first group to perform its skit. After the skit, offer positive feedback, then invite the class to suggest additional ways to handle the situation. Repeat this process for each group.

Step 11 Ask students to review their answers to the questionnaire, What Would You Do? Would anyone change any of their answers based on what they learned?

Additional Activities

- Videotape the role plays. Play tape back for students, ask them if and how they would change their responses.

- Ask students to develop a program to teach their peers how to assert and advocate for themselves effectively.

What Would You Do?

1. **You and a friend are selecting a movie to go see. You:**

   a. suggest the movie you've been dying to see
   b. allow your friend to select the movie
   c. select the movie

2. **You and a friend are supposed to go out on Friday night. Your friend wants to go to a party, but you do not. You:**

   a. go to the party because your friend really wants to go
   b. refuse to go to the party
   c. suggest that your friend go to the party Friday night and the two of you go out Saturday night

3. **You have just been given an assignment in health class that stirs up a lot of emotions for you. You:**

   a. do the assignment as requested
   b. refuse to do the assignment
   c. discuss the assignment and your feelings with the teacher

4. **Your receive a credit card bill in the mail. The bill includes items you did not purchase. You:**

   a. pay the bill
   b. throw the bill away and ignore the extra charges
   c. call the credit card company to discuss the discrepancies

5. **You just purchased an expensive sweater, which you vow to yourself not to lend out. Your friend asks to borrow it. You:**

   a. lend it to your friend
   b. tell your friend no
   c. tell your friend no and offer her another sweater

6. **A friend asks you to lie for her. You tell her you don't feel comfortable lying. She responds, "If you were my friend, you would." You:**

   a. lie for your friend
   b. refuse to lie
   c. encourage her to seek an alternate plan that does not involve you

What Would You Do? Questionnaire Outcome

After completing the scenarios on the first page, total your score as follows:

- one point for each "a" answer
- two points for each "b" answer
- three points for each "c" answer

If you scored:

- fourteen to eighteen points, you tend to be assertive
- nine to thirteen points, you tend to be aggressive
- zero to eight points, you tend to be passive

Learn To Become Assertive

"To change or not to change is a risk. You must trust and listen to yourself. Sometimes not changing is a bigger risk than change."

—Billie Jean King
Director, World Team Tennis

Being assertive means standing up for your rights without violating anyone else's rights.

Assertiveness is not the same as aggressiveness. Aggressiveness is when someone stands up for their own rights and violates others' rights.

Being assertive means:

- doing things that are good for you
- advocating for what you want and need
- displaying your true feelings
- respecting others' feelings
- being fair to yourself and others

Being assertive does not mean:

- using force
- threatening
- being sneaky

Passive, Assertive, Or Aggressive?

Passive	Assertive	Aggressive
• Go along • Say nothing	• State your needs without violating anyone else's	• Disregard the needs of others

Assertiveness Role Plays

1. You and a friend are at a party. Your curfew is at midnight. It takes twenty minutes to get from the party to your house. At 11:30, you ask your friend to take you home. She says "OK," then continues to talk and enjoy herself. At 11:40, your friend is still talking and does not appear ready to leave. What do you do?

2. You are on a date with the partner of your dreams. You go to a movie. On the way home, he or she takes a detour. You ask where you're headed, and your date says, "I thought we could be alone." You arrive at a secluded area, where your date stops the car. He or she moves closer, begins kissing you, and lets his or her hands wander. You do not feel comfortable. What do you do? What precautions can you take to prevent this situation?

3. You are completing a research paper and actively involved in choir and dormitory life. Your basketball coach asks you to organize a fund-raiser for the team. Though you are very committed to the team, your time is limited. How do you handle this situation?

4. You are in the back of a school bus or van. The coolest guy on campus is sitting next to you. He places his hand on your inner thigh. You do not feel comfortable with his hand on your leg. How do you respond?

5. You are the only female in your history class. At the beginning of class each day, two of the male students make comments about your dress or body. How do you handle this situation?

Dating and Relationships

Overview
Unit 5, Dating and Relationships, asks students to evaluate their own needs in terms of relationships. Students learn the differences between healthy and unhealthy relationships, as well as the warning signs of an abusive relationship. Students explore solutions to teen dating violence.

Objectives

Upon completion of this unit, students will be better able to:

- state the problem of domestic violence and the different forms it takes

- distinguish between healthy and unhealthy relationships

- identify the warning signs of an abusive relationship

- get support should they become involved in an unhealthy relationship

- discuss solutions to domestic violence

Materials

Handouts: Student Survey

Student Survey Answers

Healthy vs. Unhealthy Relationships

Warning Signs of Abuse

Lethality Checklist

Vocabulary A to Z

Vocabulary A to Z Answer Sheet

Displays: Statistics on teen dating violence

Cartoon, drawing, movie, show, or song depicting violence against women, with VCR or CD player for display (optional)

Resources: What Can Schools Do

Equipment: Blackboard, whiteboard, or easel with flip chart

Instructions

Step 1 Display statistics on teen dating violence around the room. Distribute all handouts for the unit, except for the Student Survey Answers and the vocabulary and definition cards.

Step 2 Ask students to complete the Student Survey. The results will give you baseline information about students' knowledge of abusive relationships.

Step 3 After students complete the survey, explain that statistics show that dating violence affects at least one in ten teen relationships. To help students avoid "becoming a statistic," this unit asks them to evaluate their needs in terms of relationships. It provides information to help students identify healthy and unhealthy relationships, as well as the warning signs of an abusive relationship.

Step 4 Distribute the handout, Student Survey Answers. Briefly discuss each statement on the Student Survey with the class and explain why it is true or false.

Step 5 Invite students to brainstorm different types of abuse (such as physical, emotional, verbal, and sexual) that can occur in an unhealthy relationship. Ask directed questions to elicit responses, if necessary.

Step 6 Divide the class into small groups. Ask the groups to use a two-column note-taking format to list the differences between healthy and unhealthy relationships. Write this example on the board:

Healthy Relationships	Unhealthy Relationships
Caring	Possessive

Groups should take about ten minutes to create their lists. Each group should select a recorder to take notes and a reporter to report the results back to the class.

Step 7 Invite the reporter from each group to report the results. As the reporters speak, write their comments on the board.

Step 8 Review the questionnaire, Warning Signs of Abuse. State that it is for students' private use. Students should complete it on their own to determine whether they are involved in an unhealthy relationship. They should not write their names on it.

At this time, you may want to review resources—people and places—for students who have concerns about their relationships or a friend's relationship (such as school counselors and outside agencies).

Step 9 Review the Lethality Checklist. Tell students that if any of the scenarios on the checklist have occurred in their present relationship that they should immediately get help. Their life or someone else's may be in immediate danger. In Massachusetts, Help for Abused Women and Their Children (HAWC) is one excellent resource. You should provide students with a list of local resources. The District Attorney's office may help direct you to programs.

Step 10 Develop a cooperative learning exercise by making cards using two different colors. Designate one color for vocabulary terms and the other color for definitions. Divide the class into two groups. Give half the students in each group the vocabulary cards and the other half the definition cards. Instruct each group to match the vocabulary words with their definitions. Please consult state laws to verify the accuracy of the definitions. The definitions provided within this guide are based on Massachusetts Law. Laws may vary from state to state.

Step 11 Review the words on the handout, Vocabulary A to Z. Students should fill in each word as you define it. State that these are common crimes committed between people. Give examples of each crime. Again, please review state laws to ensure accuracy. Laws may vary from state to state. *(What Can Schools Do to Respond?,* published by the District Attorney's office in Essex County, Massachusetts, is a useful resource. It is included for your convenience.)

Step 12 Invite students to brainstorm ideas for managing the following situations:

- If you were being abused by someone you were dating, what could you do and where could you go for help?

- If you were abusing someone you were dating, what things could you do and where could you go for help?

- If you knew someone who was in an abusive relationship, what could you do to help?

The answers to these questions and the resources (such as counselors, battered women's or domestic violence programs, the District Attorney's office, and the local police) available vary from one school, community, and locality to the next. You should research resources in your area and provide a list to the class. Alternatively, you can also have students create and distribute a resource guide as part of the unit.

Student Survey

Please do not write your name on this survey. Fill in the blank with a(n):

- T if you believe the statement is true
- F if you believe the statement is false
- U if you are uncertain about the statement

1. The media can influence a person's attitude and behavior. _____

2. Alcohol and drugs can cause someone to become violent. _____

3. Domestic violence occurs most often in the relationships of those in the lower socio-economic level. _____

4. Abuse in a relationship does not generally lead to serious injury. _____

5. If your partner wants you to stop being friends with someone, it is because he or she loves you a lot. _____

6. Most abusers abuse their partners as a way of gaining control over them. _____

7. When a person is raped, it is because he or she asked for it. _____

8. A battered woman stays with an abuser because she likes to be abused. _____

9. Children who witness domestic violence often grow up rejecting violence as adults. _____

10. A person makes the choice to become violent. _____

11. Sex between people who know one another cannot be considered rape. _____

12. When a woman says "no" to sex, she means "yes." _____

Student Survey Answers

1. **The media can influence a person's attitude and behavior.** *True*

   Our attitudes and behaviors are influenced by the media (such as television, radio, and newspapers) on a daily basis—sometimes without us even being aware of their impact. The more we are exposed to media sources, the more our behaviors and attitudes are likely to become influenced.

2. **Alcohol and drugs do not cause someone to become violent.** *True*

   Alcohol and drugs do not cause someone to become violent. A person must already have violent tendencies on which they act. Substances may cloud a person's judgment, but they cannot cause a person to become violent.

3. **Domestic violence occurs most often in the relationships of those in the lower socio-economic level.** *False*

   Domestic violence affects people at all socio-economic levels. It is not determined by financial status.

4. **Abuse in a relationship does not generally lead to serious injury.** *False*

   If abuse is allowed to continue, it generally increases in intensity and eventually results in serious injury.

5. **If your partner wants you to stop being friends with someone, it is because he or she loves you a lot.** *False*

   If your partner wants you to stop being friends with someone, it is because he or she is attempting to control you and select your friends. You are your own person and need to make decisions on your own. A loved one respects your opinion and friendships.

6. **Most abusers abuse their partners as a way of gaining control over them.** *True*

   Abusers abuse for control. They want to keep the victim at their mercy. To rope the victim back in, they convince him or her that they are sorry and that the abuse will never happen again.

7. **When a person is raped, it is because he or she asked for it.** *False*

   Rape is not a crime of passion. It is a crime of power and control. No one asks to be raped, and no one deserves it.

8. **A battered person stays with an abuser because he or she likes to be abused.** *False*

   A battered person does not enjoy the abuse. An abused person generally lacks the resources or support (such as financial resources and counseling) to leave a relationship—and in many cases a home—to stop the abuse.

9. **Children who witness domestic violence often grow up rejecting violence as adults.** *False*

   Children who witness abuse learn to abuse and generally become abusers. To break the cycle, someone needs a lot of emotional support and to learn how to deal with feelings appropriately.

10. **A person makes the choice to become violent.** *True*

    People control their own thoughts and actions. Although others may influence a person's attitudes and behavior, the individual person makes the choice to become violent.

11. **Sex between people who know one another cannot be considered rape.** *False*

    Most rapes are committed by known assailants, such as relatives and friends.

12. **When a person says "no" to sex, he or she means "yes."** *False*

    When a person says "no," he or she means "no."

Healthy vs. Unhealthy Relationships

Healthy Relationships	Unhealthy Relationships
Love	Jealousy
Responsibility	Possessiveness
Hard work	Pain
Pleasure	Violence
Commitment	Obsession
Caring	Selfishness
Honesty	Cruelty
Intimacy	Sex
Trust	Getting pregnant
Communication	Getting someone pregnant
Sharing	Dependency
Compromising	Giving up yourself
Closeness	Intimidation
Recognizing differences	Scoring
Respecting differences	Fear
Vulnerability	Proving yourself
Openness	Manipulation
Respect	Disrespect
Friendship	Expecting all your needs to be met
Strong feelings	Losing yourself

Warning Signs Of Abuse

Are you going out with someone who:

1. Is jealous and possessive toward you, won't let you have friends, checks up on you, or won't accept breaking up? _____

2. Tries to control you by being very bossy, giving orders, and making all the decisions? Doesn't take your opinions seriously? _____

3. Is scary, threatens you, or uses or owns weapons? Causes you to worry about how he or she will react to things you say or do? _____

4. Is violent, has a history of fighting, loses his or her temper quickly, or brags about mistreating others? _____

5. Pressures you for sex or is forceful or scary around sex? Thinks of women or girls as sex objects? Attempts to manipulate or guilt-trip you by saying, "if you really loved me, you would"? Grew too serious about the relationship too fast? _____

6. Abuses drugs or alcohol or pressures you to take them? _____

7. Blames you when he or she mistreats you? Says you "provoked me," "pushed my buttons," "made me do it," or "led me on"? _____

8. Has a history of bad relationships yet blames the other person for all the problems by saying things like, "girls just don't understand me"? _____

9. Believes that men should be in control and powerful and that women should be passive and submissive? _____

10. Has hit, pushed, choked, restrained, kicked, or physically abused you?

11. Your family and friends have warned you about the person? Causes your friends or family to tell you they are worried for your safety? _____

If you answered "yes" to two or more of these questions, please get help. These are warning signs of abuse. If your abuser uses drugs or weapons, it is a potentially lethal mixture. You need help immediately. Your life or someone else's may be in immediate danger.

In Massachusetts, Help for Abused Women and Their Children (HAWC) is one excellent resource. Please check your area for local resources. The District Attorney's office may help direct you to programs.

Lethality Checklist

_____ **Threats of homicide or suicide.** Batterers who have threatened to kill themselves, their partners, their children, or relatives must be considered extremely dangerous.

_____ **Fantasies of homicide or suicide.** Batterers who develop a fantasy about who, how, when, or where to kill are highly dangerous. Those who have previously acted out part of a homicide or suicide fantasy may perceive killing as a viable "solution" to their problems. As with suicide assessment, the more detailed the plan and the more available the method, the greater the risk.

_____ **Weapons.** When batterers possess weapons and have used them or threatened to use them in past assaults, access to those weapons increases the potential for lethal assault. The use of guns is a strong predictor of homicide. If a batterer has a history of arson or threatening arson, fire should be considered a weapon.

_____ **"Ownership" of the battered person.** Batterers who make statements like "death before divorce" or "you belong to me and will never belong to someone else" may be expressing a fundamental belief that their partner has no right to a separate life. Batterers who believe they are absolutely entitled to their partner and their partner's services, obedience, and loyalty—no matter what—are likely to be life-endangering.

_____ **Centrality of the partner.** People who idolize their partners, who depend heavily on them to organize and sustain their lives, or who isolate themselves from all other community may retaliate if their partner decides to end the relationship. They rationalize that the "betrayal" justifies lethal retaliation.

_____ **Separation violence.** When batterers believe they are about to lose their partner, they may choose to kill if they cannot envision life without the partner or if the separation causes them great despair or rage.

_____ **Depression.** When batterers are acutely depressed and see little hope for moving beyond the depression, they may be candidates for homicide or suicide. Research shows that many men who are hospitalized for depression have homicidal fantasies directed at family members.

_____ **Access to the partner or family members.** Batterers who cannot find their partners cannot kill them. Batterers who do not have access to their children cannot use them to gain access to their partners. Careful safety planning and police assistance are required when contact between batterer and partner is required, such as at court appearances and custody exchanges.

_____ **Repeated outreach to law enforcement.** Partner homicide almost always occurs when there has been a history of violence. Prior calls to the police indicate an elevated risk of life-threatening conduct. The more a batterer has been reported to the police, the greater the potential danger.

_____ **Escalation of batterer risk.** A less obvious indicator of increasing danger may be a sharp escalation in the amount of personal risk a batterer undertakes. When batterers begin to act without regard for the legal or social consequences that previously constrained their violence, chances of lethal assault significantly increase.

_____ **Hostage-taking.** A hostage-taker is at high risk of committing homicide. Between seventy-five and ninety percent of all hostage-takings in the United States are related to domestic violence.

Source: Hart, B. "Assessing Whether Batterers Will Kill." Pennsylvania Coalition Against Domestic Violence, 1990.

Vocabulary A To Z

A __ __ __ __ __ __

An attempt or offer to do bodily injury by force or violence or an attempt to batter

A __ __ __ __ __ __ A __ __
B __ __ __ __ __ __

A harmful or prohibited touching of another, no matter how slight, without a legal right to do so

T __ __ __ __ __ __

A verbal or written statement that a victim reasonably believes another may act upon

S __ __ __ __ __ __ __

The willful, malicious, and repeated following or harassing of an individual, including making threats with intent to place that person in imminent fear of death or serious bodily injury

I __ __ __ __ __ __ __
A __ __ __ __ __ __ A __ __
B __ __ __ __ __ __

An intentional, offensive touching of a person fourteen years of age or older without their consent

R __ __ __

Sexual intercourse or unnatural sexual intercourse committed against one's will with the use of force or the threat of bodily injury; includes penetration into any bodily orifice (mouth, anus, or vagina) by a penis, finger, tongue, or other object

S __ __ __ __ __ __ __ __
R __ __ __

Unlawful sexual intercourse or unnatural sexual intercourse with a child under sixteen years of age; a child under the age of sixteen is incapable, as a matter of the law, to consent to sexual intercourse, unless married to the partner

R __ __ __ __ __ __ __ __ __ __ __
O __ __ __ __ __

Issued by a judge through the courts; places additional limits on the interactions between two parties for protection from further abuse

Vocabulary A To Z Answer Sheet

(These definitions are based on Massachusetts laws. Laws may vary from state to state.)

ASSAULT	An attempt or offer to do bodily injury by force or violence or an attempt to batter
ASSAULT AND BATTERY	A harmful or prohibited touching of another, no matter how slight, without a legal right to do so
THREATS	A verbal or written statement that a victim reasonably believes another may act upon
STALKING	The willful, malicious, and repeated following or harassing of an individual, including making threats with intent to place that person in imminent fear of death or serious bodily injury
INDECENT ASSAULT AND BATTERY	An intentional, offensive touching of a person fourteen years of age or older, without their consent
RAPE	Sexual intercourse or unnatural sexual intercourse committed against one's will with the use of force or the threat of bodily injury; includes penetration into any bodily orifice (mouth, anus, or vagina) by a penis, finger, tongue, or other object
STATUTORY RAPE	Unlawful sexual intercourse or unnatural sexual intercourse with a child under sixteen years of age; a child under the age of sixteen is incapable, as a matter of law, to consent to sexual intercourse unless married to the partner
RESTRAINING ORDER	Issued by a judge through the courts; places additional limits on the interactions between two parties for protection from further abuse

What Can Schools Do?

What Can a School System Do to Help Protect a Student Who Has Taken Out a Restraining Order?

(Excerpt from Document prepared by the Office of the District Attorney for the Eastern District of the Commonwealth of Massachusetts)

Staff and student awareness of dating violence issues are increased through training, policy development and implementation. It is hoped that all students will have an understanding of the school's sensitivity and commitment to insure safety for students who have obtained a restraining order through the court, through the utilization of safety plans and development of protective measures in school. School systems may want to develop their policies in collaboration with the police, courts, shelter, legal advocates and the D.A.'s office. With this in mind, students should be encouraged and feel comfortable in approaching administrators to assist them in the process, so that the appropriate actions and safety planning will occur.

Once the School Is Notified of a Student's Restraining Order:

- The School administrator may want to hold **SEPARATE** meetings with each student and his/her family to gather any information, review the order and the implications.

Included as a part of this meeting should also be an agreement as to who this information will be shared with.

- A "Safety Plan" should be worked out to address the victim's needs, including "safety stops," staff to report to if concerns arise or a violation occurs, and any schedule changes that may be considered. This meeting should include a discussion of guidelines for appropriate behavior of the victim, such as not making comments to others which may inflame the situation.

- With the named defendant, it is important to review the terms of the order, expectations around appropriate behavior, and the consequences for violation of the order.

- When possible it is important to address and make schedule changes to avoid face-to-face contact. When schedule changes are not possible, guidelines should be established around expected behavior.

What Guidelines Should Be Considered?

- It is important to establish clear guidelines around expected behavior in compliance with the issued order, for the benefit and safety of all parties. These could include: delineation of space between parties (feet, yardage, routes to classes), class or schedule changes. Giving a clear message that there be no exchange (verbal or non-verbal, threatening or non-threatening) of comments, notes, gifts, gestures is critical. This also includes no exchange of messages, notes, gifts through a third party friend, student or staff member.

  NOTE: Given the reality of the close proximity within the school setting and/or the possibility of both students needing to remain in the same class, the order may need to be amended to reflect clear guidelines around contact in such instances.

- IT IS IMPORTANT TO UNDERSTAND THAT THE ONUS OF THE RESTRAINING ORDER IS ON THE DEFENDANT. A VICTIM CANNOT VIOLATE THE RESTRAINING ORDER, THOUGH REALISTICALLY, REASONABLE BEHAVIOR AND COOPERATION IS REQUIRED BY BOTH PARTIES.

What Should Happen if It Appears That the Order Is Being Violated?

- VIOLATION OF A RESTRAINING ORDER IS A CRIMINAL OFFENSE AND SHOULD BE TREATED SO, BY REPORTING IT TO THE PROPER AUTHORITIES. (Schools may want to develop their own internal reporting mechanism, but ultimately the violation must be reported to the police.)

  NOTE: It is important that the school support the victim in reporting any violations that have been witnessed or reported. The school does not need to be the judge as to the violation, but should report the violation to the proper authorities for their determination of the necessary action to be taken.

Restraining Order School Checklist

Restraining Order issued on behalf of (see attached copy of filed restraining order)

Student Name _____ Grade _____ H.R. _____

**Class Schedule (*copies of schedules attached for both victim and defendant*)

Defendant's Name _____ Grade _____ H.R. _____
(*If defendant does not attend the same school, note school attends, attach picture, description, car make, license plate #, trespassing letter sent. . .*)

Are There Any Schedule Conflicts?

Class Changes To Be Made? (Please make sure updated schedule is attached)

Meeting Date(s) NOTE: *School Administrator must hold* **separate** *meetings with the victim and defendant.*

With Victim _____
With Defendant _____
With Parents of Victim _____
With Parents of Defendant _____

REVIEW MEETING DATE(S)

_____ _____ _____

_____ _____
SCHOOL ADMINISTRATOR SIGNATURE   Date

NOTE: *The onus of the restraining order is on the defendant. A victim cannot violate the restraining order, though realistically, reasonable behavior and co-operation is expected by BOTH PARTIES.*

VIOLATION OF A RESTRAINING ORDER IS A CRIMINAL OFFENSE AND ANY VIOLATIONS SHOULD BE IMMEDIATELY REPORTED TO THE POLICE.

Teen Safety Plan

This safety plan should be considered whether or not a Restraining Order has been issued by the court.

> Student Name _____ Grade _____ H.R. _____
>
> Administrative Staff _____
>
> *(Designated administrative staff responsible for schedule changes and assessing whether or not this plan is working/or other changes need to be made)*

Safety Plan to Include The Following:

Any Schedule Changes Made (*attach revised schedule*):

_____

_____

_____

_____

School Arrival (*change in time, entrance, transportation, with whom, etc. . .*)

_____

_____

Locker

_____

_____

Lunch

_____

_____

Route Changes (*include places to avoid/watch for. . .*)

_____

_____

VIOLATION OF A RESTRAINING ORDER IS A CRIMINAL OFFENSE AND ANY VIOLATIONS SHOULD BE IMMEDIATELY REPORTED TO THE POLICE.

School Departure (*time, entrance, designated friend, etc. . .*)

_____

_____

_____

STAFF: *Designate one staff person with whom student feels comfortable. This staff person should be available for student for "check-ins" and support as needed.*

Support Staff _____

Additional Staff to Share Plan With: (Administrators, Teachers, Guidance)

_____   _____

_____   _____

_____   _____

Support Network of Peers: (*to accompany student through the day* if necessary)

_____

_____

_____

_____

Strategies To Problem Solve:

Any Additional Special Conditions:
Are there other extracurricular school activities/events which present conflicts? How are they to be addressed?

_____

_____

_____

_____

> **VIOLATION OF A RESTRAINING ORDER IS A CRIMINAL OFFENSE AND ANY VIOLATIONS SHOULD BE IMMEDIATELY REPORTED TO THE POLICE.**

Potential Problems/Problems Areas: (*Consider strategies to assess danger-ousness/threats. . .*)

_____

_____

_____

_____

NOTE: *The onus of the restraining order is on the defendant. A victim cannot violate the restraining order, though realistically, reasonable behavior and co-operation is expected by BOTH PARTIES.*

VIOLATION OF A RESTRAINING ORDER IS A CRIMINAL OFFENSE AND ANY VIOLATIONS SHOULD BE IMMEDIATELY REPORTED TO THE POLICE.

"Model" Safety Plan Implementation

Mary Lou, a sixteen year old student from Winterville attends North Vocational School in Spring Valley. A Restraining Order has been issued by the District Court against Jed, her sixteen year old ex-boyfriend, who also lives in Winterville and attends North Vocational School (which is in a different community than the students live in).

The police in Winterville issued the Restraining Order which states Jed Must

- Refrain from abuse;
- Have no contact with Mary Lou;
- Stay at least 50 yards away from Mary Lou.

Notification

The victim (Mary Lou) has notified the school authorities about the restraining order. It is recommended that the police notify the school where the victim goes that a restraining order has been issued and should consider notifying the police and school administration in the event that the student attends school in a different community.

- Schools should work closely with police departments around the process for notification paying attention to unique issues around:
  - regional schools (high schools and vocational schools)
  - private or parochial schools
  - students who attend schools or come to a school in a different community

> **VIOLATION OF A RESTRAINING ORDER IS A CRIMINAL OFFENSE AND ANY VIOLATIONS SHOULD BE IMMEDIATELY REPORTED TO THE POLICE.**

What Steps Should North Take?

1. Hold **SEPARATE** meetings with Mary Lou (victim) and Jed (defendant) to:

   • review the restraining order and ramifications;

   • clarify expectations;

   • review the school day, classes, lunch (open/closed campus situation), activities paying attention to potential conflicts, opportunities for face-to-face contact; and

   • identify schedule overlaps i.e. arrival/dismissal times, classes, lunch, before and after school activities, locker.

   Whenever possible face-to-face contact should be avoided. If changes need to be made, attention should be given to the victim's preference.

2. In meeting with Mary Lou (the victim) the school should consider:

   • helping Mary Lou identify adults within the school setting with whom she feels comfortable;

   • develop a "safety plan" which includes:

     • the schedule(s) of staff person(s) for support when needed;

     • routes to/from school;

     • routes to/from classes;

     • a support network of peers (peer to accompany her in travels through the day);

     • a discussion of potential problems/areas of concern (after-school activities, class trips, dances, etc. . .); and

   • follow-up meeting dates to review the situation and to make any necessary adjustments.

3. In meeting with Jed (defendant) the school should consider developing a checklist/plan that includes the following key points:

   • Identification of key staff to check in with daily/weekly or as needed.

- Any needed class/schedule changes, lunch, locker changes.

- Changes in arrival/departure times to/from school

- Changes in arrival/departure times to/from classes

- Clear review of expectations and consequences for any violations

- Follow-up meeting dates to review how things are working and to make any necessary adjustments.

The burden for any changes should be on the defendant, not the victim.

Sexual Responsibility

Overview

Unit 6, Sexual Responsibility, is designed to help students evaluate their relationships and make responsible choices pertaining to abstinence or sexual intimacy. Students build on the decision-making skills they learned in Unit 3, Making Decisions, and relate them to a decision about sexual activity. While students are encouraged to abstain, they are also encouraged to draw their own conclusions given all the potential consequences—including pregnancy, AIDS, and sexually transmitted diseases (STDs).

Sexual responsibility may be the toughest and most important subject taught in schools today. Young people must learn to make informed decisions about whether to have sex. They must also learn how to protect themselves from unwanted pregnancy, AIDS, and STDs. Conveying this information is the goal of this unit.

Though you will spend time describing birth control methods and protection against STDs, it is generally best to guide the class to a discussion of the decision-making process, the pros and cons of each birth control method, and the factors that might influence students' decisions.

Objectives

Upon completion of this unit, students will be better able to:

- understand that abstinence is the only method that is one hundred percent effective against pregnancy, AIDS, and STDs

- enter into a decision-making process about whether to have sex

- list alternatives to sex

- recognize societal influences to have sex (e.g., media and peers)

- describe birth control methods and ways to protect themselves from unwanted pregnancy and STDs

Landmark School, Inc.

Materials

Handouts: Ways to Build a Loving Relationship

              Ask Yourself Some Questions

              Fact or Myth?

              Fact or Myth Answer Sheet

              What May Influence Your Decision?

              Birth Control Methods

              Report Card

Displays: Facts on Teen Pregnancy

              Facts on Sexually Transmitted Diseases

              Miracle of Life and a VCR (optional)

Resources: Sample Letter to Parents

Equipment: Blackboard, whiteboard, or easel with flip chart

Instructions

Step 1   Before teaching this unit, you may want to notify parents of your intentions on this subject. A sample letter is included for your convenience.

Step 2   Display Facts on Teen Pregnancy and Facts on Sexually Transmitted Diseases. Distribute all handouts for this unit, except the Fact or Myth Answer Sheet.

Step 3   Tell students that this unit asks them to consider carefully all the consequences of an important decision that could easily change their lives. As their teacher, your job is not to influence their decision but to provide statistics and facts on issues of sexuality.

             Students must make their own decisions based on their values, moral viewpoint, religion, family background, and future goals. Rather than influence that choice, your goal is to present the consequences and alternatives so that students can make educated, well-considered decisions.

             As with all classroom discussions of sensitive issues, remind students to listen to and respect the ideas and views of their classmates. Keep in mind that many students may already have made a decision pertaining to sex and may or may not feel comfortable with it. Care should be taken to protect the feelings and sensitivities of those students.

Step 4 Invite students to reflect back on Unit 3, Making Decisions. You can briefly review the Thought Process Worksheet. Draw a thought process diagram on the board. Invite students to brainstorm positive and negative consequences of each option with regard to sex.

Step 5 Divide students into small groups. Ask each group to select a recorder and reporter. Instruct groups to brainstorm alternatives to sex to demonstrate that they care about someone.

Step 6 Invite each reporter to report the group's ideas. Write the ideas on the board.

Step 7 Explain that sexuality is part of what distinguishes us from one another. Sexuality includes how we look, act, and express ourselves. Sexuality also means sharing affection with someone we care about. Sexuality does not necessarily mean sex, nor does sex prove our love for someone.

Step 8 Ask for volunteers to read the criteria on the handout, Ways to Build a Loving Relationship. After each criterion, discuss the importance of that aspect of a relationship. Ask students to give examples of how we use verbal and non-verbal cues to communicate.

Step 9 Ask for a volunteer to read each question on the handout, Ask Yourself Some Questions. Invite students to explain the relevance of each question.

Step 10 Ask students to complete the questionnaire, Fact or Myth? Review the answers while asking students for input as to why each statement is a fact or myth. Give students in-depth information about what makes each statement a fact or myth. After the discussion, distribute the Fact or Myth Answer Sheet.

Step 11 Divide students into small groups and ask them to brainstorm factors that may influence their decision regarding sex. You may need to give them an example, such as the media, family, peers, religion, etc. Again, ask each group to select a recorder and a reporter.

Step 12   Invite each reporter to report the group's influences and how they might affect the decision process. Write the influences on the board.

Step 13   Discuss the role of an individual's perceptions as an influence on sex.

Step 14   Ask students to generate specific examples of each influence on the handout, What May Influence Your Decision? You may assign homework by asking students to bring more examples to class the next day (e.g., songs and advertisements).

Step 15   Point to the statistics you displayed on teen pregnancy and STDs. Have students read the statistics and discuss possible ways to prevent them from rising. You may want to discuss how certain beliefs or policies interfere with sexual education.

Lower level students may have difficulty relating to percentages. To ensure their comprehension, you can, for example, ask three students to stand in front of the classroom. State that one of the three students is likely to become pregnant before age twenty.

Step 16   Review each birth control method on the handout, Birth Control Methods. You can do this in at least three ways:

- You can review the methods and their effectiveness using a worksheet like Vocabulary A to Z in Unit 5, Dating and Relationships.

- You can get samples of each birth control method and explain how each is used, what it costs, and how effective it is.

- You can invite a professional sex educator to come in to discuss birth control, as well as gynecological exams.

Step 17   Invite students to discuss the grades on the handout, Report Card.

Additional Activities

- Invite teen parents to class to talk about the realities of being a teen parent.

- Invite HIV-positive speakers to talk about what it's like to live with AIDS.

- Show the video *Miracle of Life* before the questionnaire, Fact or Myth? (step 9)

Ways To Build A Loving Relationship

Sexuality is part of what separates us from others. Sexuality includes how we look, act, and express ourselves. Sexuality also means sharing affection with someone we care about. Sexuality does not necessarily mean having sex, and having sex does not prove our love for someone.

A meaningful relationship is built on four criteria:

1. Communication is expressing ourselves in the best way we can. Body language is a powerful communication tool; our bodies say a lot.

2. Acceptance is affirming one another for who we are and overlooking our partner's shortcomings.

3. Consideration is respect for our partner's opinions and desires. We should never pressure someone into doing something he or she doesn't want to do.

4. Enjoying time together means finding joy in another's company without spending a lot of money or having sex. We can show someone we care about them by:

   - talking
   - holding hands
   - hugging
   - going for a walk
   - the gift of a flower
   - writing a poem
   - singing a song
   - writing a love note
   - buying a box of candy
   - slow dancing
   - kissing
   - a soft touch
   - a warm glance
   - a surprise gift
   - sharing a private thought

Ask Yourself Some Questions

Before you make a decision about having sex, ask yourself these questions:

- Do I want to have sex for selfish reasons?
- Am I being forced to have sex?
- Will this decision affect our relationship?
- Have I thought about all of the possible consequences?
- Am I willing to accept all of the possible consequences?
- Do I have the knowledge to prevent an unwanted pregnancy and the spread of sexually transmitted diseases (STDs)?
- Can I have sex without feeling any guilt or regrets?
- Are there other ways my partner and I can build a loving relationship?
- Does this decision go against my religious beliefs?
- Have I honestly considered my values?
- Do I want to have sex because of pressure from my friends or for acceptance by my peers?
- Am I afraid I'll lose my partner if I refuse to have sex?
- Do I want to have sex to fill the emptiness?
- Do I want to have sex to rebel against my parents?

Remember, you are the only one who can answer these questions. However, you need to think about them carefully and not be afraid to ask someone for help and advice.

Source: HealthQuarters, 1998. HealthQuarters is located at 19 Broadway, Beverly, Massachusetts. Telephone (978) 922-4490.

Fact or Myth?

1. A woman can become pregnant the first time she has sex.

2. A woman cannot get pregnant if she doesn't have an orgasm.

3. A woman cannot become pregnant if she has sex during her period.

4. A woman can get pregnant if the man ejaculates just outside the vagina.

5. A woman cannot become pregnant before the onset of her period

6. Douching after sex protects a woman against pregnancy.

7. Urinating or jumping up and down after intercourse prevents pregnancy.

8. The majority of sexually active teens use birth control.

9. Condoms are nearly as effective as the Pill if used with spermicidal foam every time.

10. The Pill protects against sexually transmitted diseases (STDs).

11. Having intercourse one day may result in a pregnancy up to four days later.

12. The withdrawal method is as effective as a condom.

13. People can become infected with some STDs by sharing towels and clothes.

14. If a person has no symptoms of an STD, he or she is not infected.

Source: HealthQuarters, 1998. HealthQuarters is located at 19 Broadway, Beverly, Massachusetts. Telephone (978) 922-4490.

Fact or Myth Answer Sheet

1. A woman can become pregnant the first time she has sex.

   Fact: A woman can become pregnant any time she has unprotected intercourse. If an egg has been released and becomes fertilized by a sperm, pregnancy will occur.

2. A woman cannot get pregnant if she doesn't have an orgasm.

   Myth: Orgasm does not affect whether a woman becomes pregnant.

3. A woman cannot become pregnant if she has sex during her period.

   Myth: A woman may become pregnant any time she has unprotected sex if an egg has been released and becomes fertilized by a sperm. A woman may ovulate at any time during her cycle. A young woman who has irregular cycles has a greater chance of becoming pregnant during her period.

4. A woman can get pregnant if the man ejaculates just outside the vagina.

   Fact: Sperm present on the outside of the vagina can move up the vaginal canal and into the fallopian tubes.

5. A woman cannot become pregnant before the onset of her period.

   Myth: Some women ovulate just prior to the onset of their period. If this occurs, the egg is present and may become fertilized by a sperm.

6. Douching after sex protects a woman against pregnancy.

   Myth: Douching after sex can increase the speed of the flow of sperm to the fallopian tubes.

7. Urinating or jumping up and down after intercourse prevents pregnancy.

   Myth: Urine has no effect on whether a woman gets pregnant because it does not pass through the vagina. Jumping up and down also has no effect on the fertilization process.

8. The majority of sexually active teens use birth control.

   Myth: Nearly two-thirds of all teenage females do not use contraception on a consistent basis.

9. Condoms are nearly as effective as the Pill if used with spermicidal foam every time.

   Fact: Condoms and foam used together are ninety-five percent effective. This is slightly less effective than the Pill.

10. The Pill protects against sexually transmitted diseases (STDs).

    Myth: The Pill does not protect anyone from becoming infected with an STD. It's important to use condoms correctly and consistently to protect against STDs.

11. Having intercourse one day may result in a pregnancy up to four days later.

    Fact: Sperm can live for four to six days in the uterus or fallopian tubes. An egg can survive up to forty-eight hours. Sperm can fertilize the egg if unprotected sex occurs several days before ovulation.

12. The withdrawal method is as effective as a condom.

    Myth: The withdrawal method is ineffective as a birth control method. It is nearly impossible to keep pre-ejaculatory fluid (pre-cum) and sperm away from the vagina without a protective barrier, such as a condom.

13. People can become infected with some STDs by sharing towels and clothes.

    Fact: Scabies and pubic lice can be transmitted from towels, clothes, and bedding, as well as close physical contact. Chlamydia, genital warts, and gonorrhea, which are the most common forms of STDs, are only spread by sexual contact.

14. If a person has no symptoms of an STD, he or she is not infected.

    Myth: A person may have contracted an STD even though no symptoms have appeared.

What May Influence Your Decision?

- Lyrics to songs
- Sultry love scenes in the movies
- Peers, especially those who are sexually active
- Partners who pressure you to have sex, directly or indirectly
- A perception that sex is a way to rebel against your parents' beliefs
- Sensual advertisements
- Magazine articles and pictures that raise your curiosity
- A desire to feel needed
- Past sexual abuse
- The perception that:

  _____ everyone else is sexually active

  _____ intimacy can only be achieved through sex

  _____ your partner will leave you if you do not have sex

  _____ your partner will not leave you if you become pregnant

Birth Control Methods

1. Abstinence is not engaging in oral, anal, or vaginal intercourse. It is the only method that is one hundred percent effective against pregnancy and STDs. It is also the least expensive form of birth control.

2. Latex condoms ("rubbers") are used by the male to prevent semen from entering the vagina. Condoms can be conveniently purchased at any drugstore without a prescription. When worn properly, they can protect both partners from STDs. Condoms are eighty to ninety-five percent effective, depending on how carefully they are used. When considering the risks, the cost of condoms is minimal compared to other methods. Never use Vaseline as a lubricator for condoms. K-Y Jelly or spermicidal foam are the best choices for lubrication.

3. Birth control pills ("the Pill"), which contain the hormones estrogen and progesterone, fool a woman's body into thinking it's pregnant and thus prevent release of the egg. It does not protect either partner from STDs. The Pill can only be purchased with a prescription. The Pill must be taken every day at about the same time. When taken properly, the Pill is ninety-seven to ninety-nine percent effective in preventing pregnancy. Possible side effects include nausea, water retention, an increased risk of yeast infection, and an increase in blood pressure. Women who have cervical or breast cancer, heart or liver disorders, or a history of stroke should not take the Pill. Also, antibiotics may interfere with the Pill's effectiveness. Use of the Pill may protect against ovarian cancer.

4. Spermicidal foam (nonoxynol-9) involves inserting foam deep into the vagina no more than twenty minutes prior to sexual intercourse. The foam forms a physical barrier that kills sperm. When used alone, foam is seventy to ninety percent effective in preventing pregnancy. Foam used with a condom is ninety to ninety-nine percent effective in preventing pregnancy and is the most effective combination against STDs.

5. A diaphragm is a rubber form that fits deep inside the vagina to form a physical barrier against sperm. A cervical cap is a similar device. Either must be used with spermicidal jelly or cream. They are eighty to eighty-nine percent effective in preventing pregnancy and STDs. A physician must fit and measure a woman for a diaphragm or cervical cap, then check the

fit about once a year. A woman must check her diaphragm frequently for holes or tears. A drawback to the diaphragm is that it does not respond well to heat.

6. Norplant, intra-uterine devices (IUDs), and Depo-provera are ninety-five to ninety-nine percent effective in preventing pregnancy. Norplant is a small tubular device that is surgically implanted in a woman's arm via a small incision. An IUD is a plastic and metal device that is implanted in the uterus via the cervix. Depo-provera is an injection that a woman receives every three months. Each of these methods has possible side effects. None offers protection against STDs.

7. The female condom is relatively new to the market. Some women report that it is awkward to use. Similar to the male condom, it serves as a physical barrier to protect an egg from becoming fertilized. Its effectiveness in protecting against pregnancy and STDs is about ninety percent.

8. The withdrawal and rhythm methods are ineffective in protecting either partner from STDs. Although either is better than no method at all, their effectiveness in preventing pregnancy is extremely low at sixty-five percent. With the withdrawal method, the male withdraws from the woman's vagina prior to ejaculation. With the rhythm method, the woman carefully tracks her menstrual cycle to estimate when ovulation will occur, then avoids sex for that time (plus two or three days before and after that time as an extra precaution).

Report Card

	Protection against:	
Birth Control Method	**STDs**	**Pregnancy**
Abstinence	A +	A +
Latex condoms	B	B
Birth control pills	F	A
Spermicide (nonoxynol-9)	B	C
Diaphragm, cervical cap	B	B
Norplant, IUD, Depo-provera	F	A
Condom used with the Pill, diaphragm, cervical cap, Norplant, IUD, or Depo-provera	A	A
Female condom	B	B
Withdrawal or rhythm method	F	C
No method	F	F

When making a decision about whether to have sex and what birth control method to use, you are the only one who can make a decision that's right for you. It is your future at stake, and your future is your responsibility.

Source: HealthQuarters, 1998. HealthQuarters is located at 19 Broadway, Beverly, Massachusetts. Telephone (978) 922-4490.

Facts on Teen Pregnancy

Fifty percent of all teenage pregnancies occur within the first six months after the first act of intercourse.

Twenty percent of all teenage pregnancies occur within the first month after the first act of intercourse

One out of three women in the United States becomes pregnant before the age of twenty.

One in ten teens between the ages of fifteen and nineteen becomes pregnant every year.

Five out of every six teenage pregnancies are unintended.

Almost one in five teenage women who give birth before age seventeen experience a second birth within two years.

In 1995, youth under twenty years of age experienced over half a million births. Youth under age seventeen accounted for two hundred thousand of those births.

In 1996, twenty-two percent of all births to teenagers age fifteen to nineteen were repeat teen births. This marked a decline from twenty-five percent in 1992.

Overall abortion rates declined slightly during the early 1990s.

What can you do to avoid becoming one of these statistics?

These statistics were compiled by the Landmark School in August 1998 from these sources: Massachusetts Coalition for Pregnant and Parenting Teens; Alan Guttmacher Institute: March 1993; Sex and America's Teenagers, 1994; Center for Population Options, 1990; Child Trends, 1997.

Facts on Sexually Transmitted Diseases

The spread of STDs is epidemic in the United States. Consider:

- Twelve million new cases of STDs are diagnosed each year.

- Four million new cases of chlamydia are diagnosed each year.

- Forty million people have genital herpes, with nearly half a million new cases each year.

- Forty thousand cases of HIV and AIDS are diagnosed each year.

- AIDS is the fifth leading cause of death among adults age twenty-five to forty-four.

- Nearly ninety percent of all adults newly infected with HIV acquired the infection through heterosexual sex.

- Three million teens will be diagnosed with an STD this year. Many will go undiagnosed and untreated.

- Women, youth, and children represent a greater portion of the population infected with HIV.

- The number of AIDS cases contracted through heterosexual intercourse increased by one hundred and thirty percent from 1992 to 1993.

- The number of female teens with AIDS is nearly four times higher than among female adults.

- Youth aged thirteen to twenty-four accounted for four percent of the AIDS cases and fifteen percent of the HIV infection cases reported from 1997 to 1998.

- Intravenous drug users and men who have sex with men continue to be among the high-risk populations for HIV.

Sources: These statistics were compiled by the Landmark School in May 1998 from these sources: NEA Today, March 1995; Centers for Disease Control, 1993 and 1998; Massachusetts Department of Public Health, March 1994; World Health Organization, 1993.

Sample Letter to Parents

Date

Dear Parent or Guardian:

In March, Landmark will introduce a curriculum on Sexual Responsibility to all students. The curriculum will be presented by a trained health professional. It will include information on preventing and detecting sexually transmitted diseases. In addition, students will attend a presentation on [DATE] addressing adolescent health issues and the importance of pelvic exams and self-breast exams for females.

At Landmark, we are very clear and serious about advocating sexual abstinence, though we know many adolescents choose not to abstain. Our presenter also advocates abstinence. The curriculum involves students in a role play that includes a decision to abstain. It discusses the importance of careful, informed decision-making and developing strategies to follow through.

National statistics show that adolescents are at high risk for contracting a sexually transmitted disease. A "typical" student has sex by age sixteen. In 1991, Massachusetts reported that more than four thousand teenagers between ages fifteen and nineteen were infected and diagnosed with a sexually transmitted disease. These statistics do not include the number of adolescents with HIV. The numbers continue to rise as more and more teenagers become sexually active.

At Landmark, we strive to give our students the information and knowledge they need to exercise good judgment in their decisions. Students need to be informed of the responsibility and risks involved in becoming sexually active. They need to be prepared to make educated decisions regarding their behavior.

As a parent, as your child's primary educator, and as a resource to our school's programs, it is essential that you be comfortable with the subject matter. If you have any questions or comments, please feel free to contact me.

Sincerely,

Cheryl K. Iannucci

Assistant Dean of Students

Substance Use and Abuse

Overview

Unit 7, Substance Use and Abuse, examines individual and societal attitudes toward substance use. Students identify social pressures to use substances and skills needed to resist. Students also explore alternatives to substance use and solutions to substance abuse.

Objectives

Upon completion of this unit, students will be better able to:

- describe societal attitudes towards substance use
- identify social pressures to use substances
- implement social resistance skills to avoid substance use while maintaining friendships
- list alternatives to substance use
- state that most people do not use substances
- evaluate their own substance use or abuse

Materials

Handouts: What Is Adolescence?

Developmental Influences on an Adolescent

Ask Yourself Some Questions

Social Influences on Substance Use

Resisting Social Influences

Effects of Substance Use

Reasons Not to Use Substances

Indicators of Substance Abuse

Alternatives to Substance Use

Landmark School, Inc.

Displays: Facts About Substances

A song that addresses substance use, with equipment to play it

Equipment: Blackboard, whiteboard, or easel with flip chart

Instructions

Step 1   Display Facts About Substances. Distribute all handouts for the unit.

Step 2   Begin by inviting students to brainstorm societal pressures that may influence someone to use substances. Write students' inputs on the blackboard. Tell students that this unit asks them to consider their decisions about substance use carefully. It offers specific methods for making a well-considered decision that best meets their individual needs. Everyone is encouraged to participate in discussions. Emphasize the necessity of sensitivity to others' feelings and respect for others' comments.

Step 3   Briefly explain the displayed statistics on adolescent substance use, Facts About Substances, emphasizing the number of people who do not use substances.

Step 4   Briefly discuss the handout, What Is Adolescence? Invite student feedback. Refer to the handout, Developmental Influences on an Adolescent. Invite students to share those influences they are experiencing (e.g., independence and body image).

Explain that these two handouts identify key aspects of the adolescent development process. Ask students how these aspects compare with adulthood, using their parents as an example. Tell students that substance abuse stops the development process. Abusers cease their progress toward adulthood until they discontinue use.

Step 5   Refer students to Unit 3, Making Decisions. Ask them to review the decision-making process. Then ask students to review the questions on the worksheet, Ask Yourself Some Questions, and to complete a Thought Process Worksheet using the questions as a guideline.

Step 6   Divide students into small groups. Ask groups to brainstorm social influences on substance use (e.g., family and self-esteem) and how each influences us. Ask each group to select a recorder and a reporter. Review the handout, Social Influences on Substance Use.

Step 7   Invite each reporter to present the group's ideas. Using a two-column note-taking format, write the type of influence and how it influences substance use.

Step 8   Ask groups to take the assignment a step further and identify ways to avoid or resist each type of influence. Invite each reporter to report the group's ideas. Take notes on the board. Review the handout, Resisting Social Influences.

Step 9   Divide students into small groups. Assign a recorder and reporter in each group. Ask groups to brainstorm creative ways to refuse alcohol, tobacco, and other drugs. The recorder should writer down each "turn-down" strategy. Invite each reporter to list the strategies the group developed.

The age and temperament of the class determine how to best run this exercise. Some students may need help developing comfortable language to say "no." Your job is to coach them on appropriate, effective language. For example, a shy child might want to say, "No, thanks" or "I have to go." A more socially adept student may say, "No, I don't do drugs."

Step 10   Review the handouts, Effects of Substance Use and Reasons Not to Use Substances.

Step 11   Lead a discussion of the negative consequences, including the legal consequences and ramifications, that can result from substance use (e.g., date rape). You may want to mention rohypnol (the "date rape pill") briefly. Take notes on the board.

Step 12   Review the handout, Indicators of Substance Abuse. Emphasize that a student who identifies with the CAGE test should consult with a family member, counselor, or trusted adult. A decision not to seek help could have serious consequences.

Step 13   Review the handout, Alternatives to Substance Use. Ask students to brainstorm additional alternatives. Take notes on the board.

Step 14   Ask the class to plan and organize a substance-free activity for the class or school (e.g., a dance or bowling night).

What Is Adolescence?

Ambivalent — changing best friends and partners

Distancing yourself from your parents

Occupation — thinking about what you want to do or getting a job

Lonely — feeling like you can't talk to your parents or other adults

Ego — developing an identity

Sexual experimentation

Conceptualizing — thinking deep thoughts

Egocentric — self-centered or "me" thinking

Narcissistic — an "I know" attitude

Communication frenzy

Experimentation — with everything

—Unknown author

Developmental Influences on An Adolescent

- Body image/physical appearance
- Friends/partners
- Sexuality
- Culture
- Clothing/fads
- Fitting in
- Independence/dependence
- Experimentation
- Cars

Ask Yourself Some Questions

Before you make a decision regarding substance use, ask yourself:

- Why would I want to use substances?

- Have I considered all the possible consequences?

- Am I willing to accept all of the possible consequences?

- Will a decision to use substances affect my relationship with anyone else (e.g., friends and parents)?

- Do I know the physical and psychological effects of the substance I'm thinking of using?

- Can I make a decision to use substances without any guilt or regrets?

- Does a decision to use substances go against my values or morals?

- Do I want to take substances because of pressure from my friends?

- Am I being forced to use substances?

- Do I want to take substances to avoid handling a conflict or uncomfortable feelings?

- Am I trying to become someone I'm not?

- What are better ways of accomplishing similar goals?

You are the only one who can answer these questions. Please evaluate your answers carefully and don't be afraid to ask someone for help or advice.

Social Influences on Substance Use

- A family member may use substances heavily.

- Certain cultures support heavy use of substances, such as alcohol.

- Alcohol advertisements display people drinking and "having fun."

- Some movies may make substance use appear "cool."

- Songs may glorify the use of substances.

- Peers may use and encourage you to join them; no one likes to use alone.

- People with poor self-esteem may use to feel better about themselves or increase their self-confidence.

- Some people believe use will enhance their abilities to perform certain tasks, such as social interactions.

- People who are unable to handle conflict or manage their anxiety may use to avoid uncomfortable feelings.

- Boredom—the feeling that there is nothing else to do—may cause people to use.

- Some people inherit a tendency to become addicted. These people are genetically predisposed to addiction.

Resisting Social Influences

- If a member of your family is addicted, take action now by:

  ___ talking with a professional (e.g., substance abuse counselor, physician, or mental health professional)

  ___ joining a support group (e.g., Al-Anon is a support group for members to help one another deal with the problems of having a relative who is addicted to substances)

  ___ taking yourself off the hook, because you are not responsible for someone else's addiction

- If your cultural beliefs influence you to use alcohol or other substances, you can:

  ___ talk with people within your culture about alternatives

  ___ determine whether the belief is real or perceived; the elders in your culture may help

- Don't be fooled by the "fun" activities in alcohol advertisements. Most of them would be dangerous in combination with substances.

- Movies serve one purpose: entertainment. Most are fictitious. Very rarely does reality match what's portrayed in the movies. Don't let yourself be influenced by the messages in movies.

- Song lyrics reflect one individual's perceptions or personal beliefs. Do not let a song influence your decisions. Evaluate every situation for yourself.

- If your peers use substances, you can:

  ___ explain your feelings without being judgmental about their use

  ___ suggest alternative activities that do not involve substances

  ___ meet up with your friends before or after they've used substances

  Some of your peers may become heavily involved with substances. Most likely, these people will not refrain from using around you. It is up to you to decide whether you should continue spending time with them.

A true friend without an addiction will consider your feelings and respect your decision. A friend who does not respect your decision is either not much of a friend or experiencing an addiction.

- If you're considering using substances to boost your self-esteem or to enhance your abilities, you'll be far better off:

  ___ participating in an activity you do well

  ___ building on your strengths

  ___ seeking help from a counselor to improve your self-esteem and confidence

  ___ exercising to become mentally as well as physically fit

- If your inability to handle conflict or manage anxiety is causing you to consider using, you can:

  ___ determine the cause of the conflict or anxiety and explore alternatives

  ___ ask a friend, parent, or counselor for advice or help

  ___ seek assistance from a school or community conflict resolution program

- If you're considering use of substances due to boredom, you can:

  ___ create alternative opportunities for yourself

  ___ become involved in school or community activities

  ___ take up a hobby or get a job

  ___ ask a friend, parent, or counselor for advice or support

- If you think you are genetically predisposed to addiction, you can:

  ___ join a support group

  ___ talk to a substance abuse specialist, physician, or counselor

  ___ completely avoid use of substances and seek support

Can you think of other ways to resist social pressures to use substances?

Effects Of Substance Use

- Poor mental health; psychosis; paranoia
- Poor diet
- Lack of exercise; lack of sleep
- Loss of control over life issues; crisis orientation
- Irresponsible behavior; lack of self-discipline
- Unstructured lifestyle; issues with authority
- Immediate gratification; emotional immaturity
- Rationalization and manipulation
- Decreased motivation for schoolwork and school-related activities
- Withdrawal/isolation from friends or classmates; change in peer group affiliations
- Possible overdose
- Possible death

Reasons Not to Use Substances

- Illicit drug use is illegal
- Alcohol use is illegal for those under age twenty-one.
- Substance use may lead to suspension or expulsion from school
- A conviction of possession might hamper future education and job opportunities.
- While substance use may temporarily make you feel like part of a crowd, true friendship doesn't depend on whether you go along with the crowd.
- While some young people do drugs, most young people do not.
- Substance use may make you feel good temporarily, but it often decreases interest and motivation in the primary areas of life.
- Substance use can cause health-related issues (e.g., brain damage and heart problems).
- Substance use can lead to addiction.
- Substance use can lead to death.

Indicators of Substance Abuse

The CAGE test:

Change in use

Attitude is defensive

Guilt over use or the results of use

Early morning use

If you identify with any of these aspects in your use of substances, you should consult with a family member, counselor, or trusted adult.

Alternatives to Substance Use

Have you ever heard yourself complaining about being bored or having nothing to do?

Have you ever used boredom as an excuse to use substances?

Are you ready to consider alternatives to substance use?

If your answer to any of these questions is "yes," please read on.

- Go see a movie with a friend.
- Get actively involved in school activities (e.g., sports and clubs).
- Get actively involved in the community (e.g., volunteer organizations and gyms).
- Plan substance-free parties and dances.
- Exercise! Exercise increases your motivation and makes you feel better about yourself. It's a great stress reliever, too.
- Take a walk on the beach.
- Go to a local amusement park.
- Visit the local museums.
- Get a part-time job.
- Learn a new activity (e.g., rollerblading and karate).

Can you think of other alternatives to using substances?

Facts About Substances

- Young people who use tobacco are more likely than others to use and abuse alcohol or other substances.

- Young people who use substances are more likely to become victims or perpetrators of violence, engage in unplanned and unprotected sex, experience school failure, or be seriously injured as a result of driving, or other high-risk behavior, while under the influence of substances.

- Compared to previous years, fewer people today understand the harm associated with substance use.

- In 1997, twenty-three percent of eighth-graders tried marijuana at least once. By tenth grade, twenty-one percent used marijuana within the last month.

- In 1997, nearly fifty percent of twelfth-graders surveyed had tried marijuana at least once, and about twenty-four percent used it within the last month.

- There are more harmful forms of substances, especially marijuana, available today than in the 1960s. Stronger substances have more harmful effects.

- Substances, including marijuana, have adverse effects on the skills used for driving a car (e.g., reaction time and concentration).

- Marijuana is the most frequently used illegal drug in the United States.

- Youth between the ages of twelve and seventeen report the average age they first tried marijuana was fourteen years old.

- In 1997, five to ten million people between ages twelve and seventeen are using alcohol, tobacco, or illicit drugs. This represents half of all kids this age.

Source: U.S. Department of Health and Human Services, 1997 and 1998.